Shells! Shells!

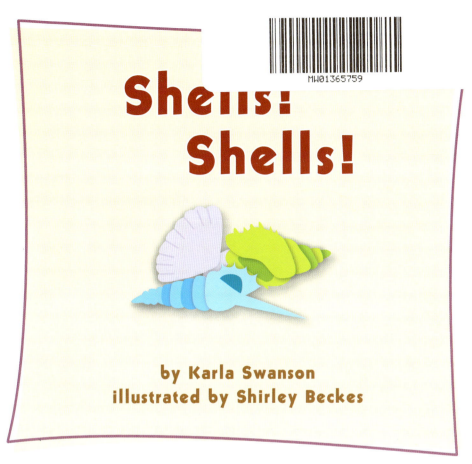

by Karla Swanson
illustrated by Shirley Beckes

 HOUGHTON MIFFLIN   BOSTON

Copyright © by Houghton Mifflin Company. All rights reserved.

No part of this work may be reproduced or transmitted in any form or by any means, electronic or mechanical, including photocopying or recording, or by any information storage or retrieval system without the prior written permission of Houghton Mifflin Company unless such copying is expressly permitted by federal copyright law. Address inquiries to School Permissions, Houghton Mifflin Company, 222 Berkeley Street, Boston, MA 02116.

Printed in China

ISBN 10: 0-618-88633-8
ISBN 13: 978-0-618-88633-3

11 12 13 14 15 0940 20 19 18 17 16 15

4500534886

 Who has more shells?
 We have the same number.

Does 1 fish have more?

 My shells are different sizes.
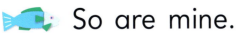 So are mine.

How can they sort the shells?

 I have 2 little shells.
I have 1 little shell.

How many little shells are there in all?

 I have 2 big shells.
 I have 1 big shell.

How many big shells are there in all?

 We have 3 big shells.
 We have 3 little shells.

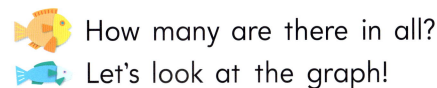 How many are there in all?
Let's look at the graph!

Problem Solving

Drawing Boxes

Draw
1. Draw 3 little shells.
2. Draw 3 big shells.

Tell About Summarize
1. Tell someone about your picture.
2. Tell about the size of the shells. Use the words *big* and *little*.

Write
1. Write about your picture.
2. Tell how many shells you drew.